Bob's Big Boy

Collectibles and Price Guide

Roy & Terry Dayton

About the authors

Roy and Terry Dayton have been collecting antiques and collectibles their whole lives. They spend their time together going to garage sales, estate sales and antique auctions. Terry always jokes with her husband Roy that they should open an antique store but in order to do that they would need to sell some of the items they collect. They refer to their home as the black hole- what comes in never goes out.

Dedication

We would like to dedicate this book to
all the Bobs Big Boy fans.

The text and products pictured in this book are from the personal collections of the authors of this book. This book is not sponsored, endorsed or otherwise affiliated with any of the companies whose products are shown. This book is derived from the authors independent research. This book does not contain all item manufactured for Bob's Big Boy and approximate prices were obtained from auction sites and past experience of purchases

Introduction

When we think of Bobs Big Boy we think of old fashioned car hops, burgers, fries, thick shakes, family and cool cars. Bobs Big Boy was started in 1936 in Glendale, California by Robert C. Wian and was originally called Bob's Pantry Restaurant. He sold his car to purchase the restaurant which at that time was a 10 seat lunch counter on Colorado Blvd in California that was abandoned when he purchased it. He had owned the restaurant for 6 months when a tipsy band member came in and requested Bob to make him something special. He split the bun in half lengthwise and invented the double decker burger. The burger was named a few weeks later when a chubby kid came into his place and he called out to the kid "Hi there Big Boy" and the idea hit him to call the burger that.

In 1949. The Bob's Big Boy on Riverside Drive was built. It is now the oldest Bobs Big Boy around. You can still drive by on a Friday night to a array of classic cars and enjoy a burger, fries and shake.

TABLE OF CONTENTS

ADVERTISEMENTS

1970's Advertisement
approx value $5-$15

1970's Hanging Cardboard lunch
box advertisement
Approx value $15-$35

1950's Drive in and
Delivery service card
Approx value $35-$50

1970's Hanging
Cardboard
Advertisement approx
value $15-$45

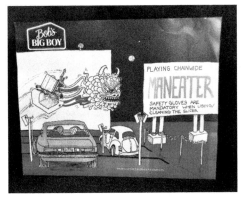

1970's Employee safety poster
Approx value$10-$35

1970's USO Advertisement
Approx Value $5-$15

1980's Advertisement
approx value
$15-$45

1986 Advertisement for
50th Anniversary glass
approx value
$15-$35

1990's Advertisement for
Neon Writers Pens
approx value
$200-$300

1956-68 Advertisement
for salad dressing
approx value
$100-$165

1970's Advertisement for cup
approx value
$35-$50

1990's Advertisement for
Time Capsules
approx value
$200-$300

1970's Advertisement
for Senior Card
approx value
$15-$30

1980's Advertisement for
Monday Night Football
approx value
$5-$15

1970's Advertisement for
Raiders Cup
approx value
$125-$225

1980's Advertisement
for cap
approx value
$15-$35

1970's Advertisement
for Buttons
approx value
$15-$30

1980's Advertisement for
Shovel and Bucket
approx value
$35-$50

1970's Advertisement for shakes and Coffee
approx value $15-$35

1980's Advertisement for Fun Racers
approx value $45-$65

1970's Advertisement and Coupon holder for Dressing
approx value $65-$85

1988-96 Hanging Advertisement
approx value $225-$265

1970's Advertisement for Fudge Brownie
approx value $5-$8

1956-68's Advertisement for Shrimp and Sauce
approx value $85-$125

1980's Advertisement
approx value $5-$15

1980's Advertisement
approx value $5-$15

1990's Advertisement
approx value $15-$25

1990's Advertisement
approx value $15-$25

1990's Advertisement
approx value $45-$65

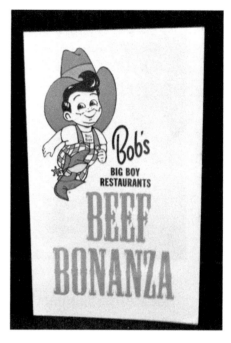

1970's Advertisement
approx value $20-$35

1980's Advertisement for
Bobs Big Boy Cap
approx value $30-$45

1980's Advertisement for
Bobs Big Boy Cap
approx value $30-$45

1980's Advertisement
approx value $50-$65

1990's Advertisement for
Bobs Big Boy Figures
approx value $60-$85

1990's Advertisement for Bobs Big Boy Figures
approx value $60-$85

1990's Advertisement for
Bobs Big Boy Figures
approx value $60-$85

1990's Advertisement
for Olympus Camera
approx value $5-$15

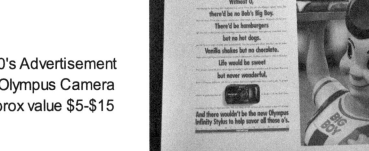

1980's Advertisement
made of heavy Plastic
approx value $15-$25

1980's Advertisement
made of heavy Plastic
approx value $15-$25

1979 Advertisement Kit
approx value $200-$250

1960's Advertisement of
Restaurant Locations
approx value $45-$60

ASHTRAYS

1956-68 Glass Ashtray
approx value $25-$45

1970's Glass ashtray
approx value $15-$35

1970's Glass Ashtray
approx value $15-$35

1990's Glass Ashtray
approx value $15-$35

1990's Glass Ashtray
approx value $15-$35

1969-87 Glass Ashtray
approx value $15-$35

1956-68 Glass Ashtray
approx value $25-$45

1969-87 Glass Ashtray
approx value $15-$35

1940's Ceramic Ashtray
approx value $500-$800

1930's Ceramic Ashtray
approx value $500-$800

1960's Glass Ashtray or
Candy dish 4"x8"
approx value $45-$65

1960's Glass Ashtray or
Candy dish 2 1/2"
approx value $45-$65

1950's Ceramic Ashtray
Made in Japan
approx value $100-$225

1969-87 Glass Ashtray or
Candy Dish 4x8"
approx value $40-$65

16

1969-87 Glass Ashtray
approx value $15-$35

1956-68 Glass Ashtray
approx value $15-$35

1969-87 Glass Ashtray
approx value $15-$35

1956-68 Glass Ashtray
approx value $25-$35

1990's Glass Ashtray
approx value $15-$35

1990's Glass Ashtray
approx value $15-$35

1969-87 Glass Ashtray
approx value $15-$35

1990's Glass Ashtray
approx value $15-$35

1956-68 Glass Ashtray
approx value $35-$65

17

BANKS

1987-96 Rubber Bank
approx value $15-$25

1987-96 Rubber Bank
approx value $15-$25

1987-96 Rubber Bank
approx value $15-$25

1956-68 Plaster Bank
approx value $225-$325

1956-68 Rubber Bank
approx value $20-$30

1956-68 Rubber Bank
approx value $20-$30

1956-68 Rubber Bank
approx value $20-$30

1969-87 Rubber Bank
approx value $25-$35

1956-68 Rubber Bank
approx value $20-$30

1956-68 Chalk Bank approx
value $1500-$2500

1970's Bank in Bag
approx value $15-$25

1987-86 bank in Box
approx value $8-$15

1970's Bank with Bobs written
in Script
approx value $8-$15

BIRTHDAY CLUB

1970's Advertisement
approx value $15-$45

1990's Party Favors
approx value $10-$20

1980's Party Hat
approx value $10-$20

1980's Party Giant Card
11"x16"
approx value $25-$55

BOBBLE HEADS

1990's Bobble head
small 4" tall
approx value $5-$15

1950's Bobble head
approx value $225-$800

1990's Bobble head 7"
approx value $5-$15

BOOKLETS, CERTIFICATES AND CATALOGS

1990's Certificate of
achievement
approx value $10-$20

1990's Kids Award
approx value $5-$15

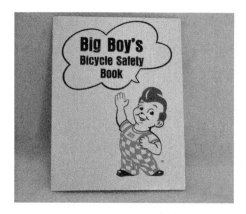

1956-68 Bicycle safety
book
approx value $85-$125

1980's Catalog
approx value $5-$15

1990's Bravery Award
approx value $5-$15

1990's Award
approx value $5-$15

1990's Passport Booklet
approx value $5-$15

1960's Advertisement
approx value $35-$45

1960's Big Boy Restaurant
Tour Book
approx value $85-$150

1990's Fun club with
Bookmark
approx value $5-$15

23

CAMPAIGN

1990's Voting Ballot
approx value $15-$25

1990's Poster
approx value $65-$125

1990's Styrofoam hat
approx value $125-$300

1990's Ballot Book
approx value $50-$125

1990's Button-Pin
approx value $5-$15

1990's Banner
approx value $150-$225

1980's Advertisement
approx value $50-$65

1990's Advertisement
approx value $15-$25

1990's Table Tent
approx value $15-$25

1990's Table Tent
approx value $15-$25

1990's Cardboard
Campaign Booth
approx value $400-$800

CARDS

1960's Deck of Cards
approx value $65-$125

1969-87 Deck of Cards
approx value $25-$45

1990's Go Fish Card
approx value $5-$15

Inside of Go Fish Cards

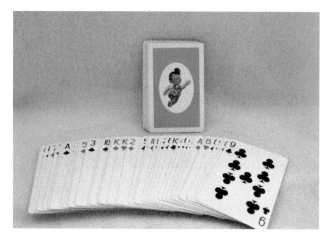

1969-87 Deck of Cards
approx value $25-$45

1990's Old Maid Card
approx value $5-$15

1990's Deck of Card
approx value $5-$15

1990's Deck of Cards
approx value $5-$15

1956-68 Deck of Cards
approx value $45-$65

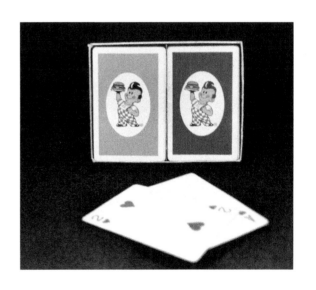

1956-68 Dual Deck Of
Cards
approx value $85-$125

CHRISTMAS ITEMS

1990's Glass Ornament
approx. value $25-$45

1956-69 Card with Ornament
approx. value $65-$85

1990's Plastic Ornament
approx. value $5-$15

1969-87 Xmas Card
approx. value $15-$20

1990's Card With Glass
Ornament
approx. value $25-$45

1988-96 Xmas Card
approx. value $15-$25

1990's Xmas Card
approx. value $15-$25

1969-87 Large Advertisement
approx. value $285-$325

1990's Gift Card Envelope
approx. value $45-$65

29

1990's Glass
approx. value $8-$15

1990's Glass
approx. value $8-$15

1969-87 Advertisement
approx. value $325-$385

1990's Glass
approx. value $8-$15

1990's Xmas Hat
approx. value $45-$65

CLOCKS AND THERMOMETERS

1970's Windup Alarm Clock
Given to Corporate members
approx value $225-$400

1990's Alarm Clock
approx value $25-$45

1980's Wall Clock
approx value $45-$65

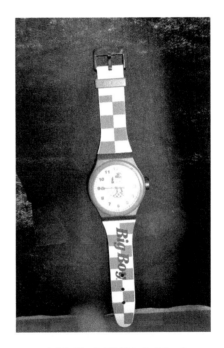

1990's 36" Wall Clock
approx value $65-$125

1997 Thermometer made
by Wolfe Studios
approx value $300-$500

1990's Wall Clock
approx value $175-$250

1990's Thermometer
approx value $25-$45

1988-96 Wall Clock
approx value $85-$125

1990's Ceramic Clock
approx value $185-$250

1970's Wall Clock
approx value $45-$75

CLOTHING AND HATS

1980's Baseball Hat
approx value $10-$25

1980's Baseball Hat
approx value $10-$25

1980's Baseball Hat
approx value $10-$25

1980's Baseball Hat
approx value $10-$25

1990's Baseball Hat
approx value $10-$25

1990's Baseball Hat
approx value $10-$25

1990's Baseball Hat
approx value $10-$25

1990's Baseball Hat
approx value $10-$25

1990's Baseball Hat
approx value $10-$25

1980's Baseball Hat
approx value $10-$25

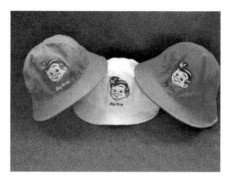

1990's Beach Hat
approx value $10-$25

1990's Baseball Hat
approx value $10-$25

1990's Baseball Hat
approx value $10-$25

1990's Baseball Hat
approx value $10-$25

1980's LA Raiders- Big
Boy Foam Hat
approx value $10-$25

1980's polo Shirt
Strawberry Festival
approx value $15-$35

1980's long sleeve shirt
approx value $15-$35

1990's Baby Bib
approx value $5-$35

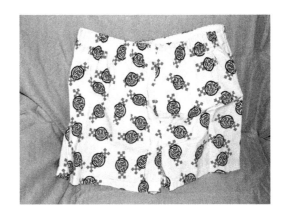

1980's Boxers
approx value $15-$35

1980's Apron
approx value $15-$45

1980's Apron
approx value $15-$45

1990's Quilt Block
approx value $120-$175

1990's Beach Towel
approx value $15-$35

1960's Uniform Shirt
approx value $125-$185

1990's Pillow Case
approx value $15-$35

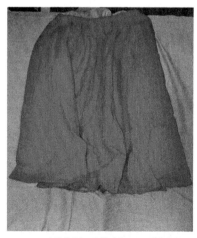

1960's Uniform Skirt
approx value $120-$185

1990's Tie
approx value $15-$35

COINS AND TOKENS

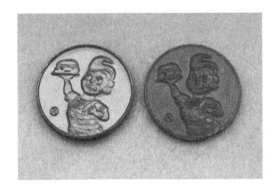 

1956-69 Assorted Plastic Tokens
approx value $4-$8

1970's Pressed Penny
approx value $15-$35

1960's Coffee Token
approx value $35-$65

COLORING, COMIC AND PUZZLE BOOKS

1990's Paint Book
approx value $3-$5

1960's Coloring Book
approx value $15-$35

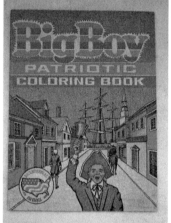

1970's Coloring Book
approx value $15-$30

1990's Magazine
approx value $3-$5

1990's Menu fun book
approx value $10-$20

1990's Menu Fun Book
approx value $10-$20

3990's Menu Puzzle Book
approx value $10-$20

1960's to Current Comic Books
approx value $1-$1000

1990's Comic Book
approx value $5-$15

1990's Menu fun book
With Adam West
approx value $10-$20

1990's Menu fun book
approx value $10-$20

1990's menu magazine
With Rosie Odonnell
approx value $5-$15

1970's Comic Book
approx value $1-$8

1990's Menu fun book
approx value $10-$20

1990's Menu Fun Book
approx value $10-$25

1990's Menu Fun Book
approx value $10-$25

1990's Menu Fun Book
approx value $10-$25

COOKIE JARS

1990's Wolfe Studios
Cookie Jar 250 made
approx value $200-$300

1990's Wolfe Studios
Cookie Jar 250 made
approx value $200-$300

1990's Wolfe Studios
Cookie Jar 250 made
approx value $200-$300

1990's Wolfe Studios
Cookie Jar 250 made
approx value $200-$300

1990's Wolfe Studios
Cookie Jar 250 made
approx value $200-$300

1990's Wolfe Studios
Cookie Jar 8 made
approx value $1000-$3500

1990's Cookie Jar
approx value $150-$250

1990's Cookie Jar
approx value $150-$250

COUPONS AND CERTIFICATES

1970's Coupon
approx value $5-$25

1970's Coupon
approx value $15-$25

1990's Gift Club
approx value $5-$15

1980's Free Burger Coupon
approx value $5-$10

1986 Glass Rain Check
Coupon
approx value $20-$125

1980's Free Burger Coupon
approx value $5-$10

1980's Advertisement
approx value $50-$65

1980's Advertisement
approx value $50-$65

1970's Coupon
approx value $50-$65

1970's Gift Coupon Book
approx value $15-$45

1970's Gift Coupon Book
approx value $15-$45

1990's Coupon Card
approx value $5-$15

1970's Unused Gift
Coupon Book
approx value $85-$100

COUPON HOLDER

1970's Cardboard
Salad dressing Coupon Holder
approx value $65-$125

1970's Cardboard
Salad dressing Coupon Holder
approx value $65-$125

1980's Advertisement
approx value $50-$65

CUPS, MUGS AND DISH-WARE

1990's Kids meal cup
approx value $4-$10

1969-87 Paper Cup
approx value $10-$25

1956-68 Paper Cup
approx value $25-$35

1956-69 Paper coffee cup
approx value $25-$35

1990's Plastic Cup
approx value $5-$15

1988-90 Paper Cup
approx value $5-$15

1956-68 Paper Cup
approx value $25-$35

1969-87 Paper Cup
approx value $5-$15

1956-68 Ice Cream Cup
approx value $5-$15

1956-68 Ice Cream Cup
approx value $15-$25

1990's Paper Cup
approx value $5-$15

1990's Paper Cup
approx value $5-$15

1990's Plastic Kids Cup
approx value $5-$15

1990's Plastic Kids Cup
approx value $5-$15

1990's Plastic Kids Cup
approx value $5-$15

1990's Plastic Kids Cup
approx value $5-$15

1990's Plastic Kids Cup
approx value $5-$15

1990's Plastic Kids Cup
approx value $5-$15

1990's Sippy Cup
approx value $10-$20

1990's Sippy Cup
approx value $10-$20

1990's Sippy Cup
approx value $10-$20

1990's Sippy Cup
approx value $10-$20

1990's Sippy Cup
approx value $10-$20

1990's Sippy Cup
approx value $10-$20

1990's Sippy Cup
approx value $10-$20

1990's Styrofoam Cup
approx value $5-$10

1990's Plastic Cup
approx value $5-$15

1990's Plastic Cup
approx value $5-$15

1969-87 Plastic Cup
approx value $25-$45

1990's Plastic Cup
approx value $5-$15

1990's Plastic Coffee Cup
approx value $5-$15

1990's Plastic Cup
approx value $5-$15

1969-87 Paper Cup
approx value $15-$25

1990's Sipper Cup
approx value $5-$15

1990's Squeezer Bottle
approx value $5-$15

1990's Hawaii
Glass Coffee Cup
approx value $5-$15

1980's Evolution
Glass Coffee Cup
approx value $20-$30

1970's Glass
Coffee Cup
approx value $25-$35

1990's Glass
Large Mug
approx value $15-$20

1970's Plastic
Coffee Cup
approx value $50-$65

1970's Canoga Park, Ca
Coffee Mug
approx value $25-$35

1980's Evolution Glass
approx value $15-$25

1990's Christmas Glass
approx value $4-$8

1940's Gold rimmed Glass
approx value $150-$250

1990's Shot Glass
approx value $12-$18

1969 Short blue logo glass
approx value $15-$20

1969 Tall Blue Glass Rack
approx value $25-$45

1969 Tall Blue Logo Glass
approx value $20-$35

1980's Coffee Mug-Hesperia
approx value $12-$18

1980's Coffee Mug-Burbank
approx value $12-$18

1980's Coffee Mug
approx value $12-$18

1980's Coffee Mug
Approx value $12-$18

1980's Mug w/Pewter Logo
approx value $35-$50

1986 Anniversary Glass
approx value $4-$8

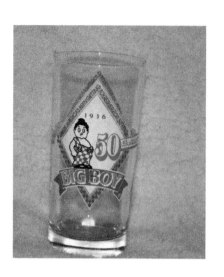

1986 50th Anniversary glass
approx value $4-$8

1970's Parfait Glass
approx value $15-$25

1970's Champagne Goblet
approx value $15-$25

1970's Wine Goblet
approx value $15-$25

1970's Goblet
approx value $15-$25

1980's Etched Glass
approx value $30-$45

1990's Plastic Coffee Mug
approx value $12-$18

1969-87 Plastic Cup
approx value $12-$18

1970's and 1990 Child's Sippy Cup t
approx value $12-$18

1990's Child's Sippy Cup
approx value $12-$18

1990's Plastic Coffee Pot
approx value $15-$25

1960's Oval Plate
approx value $75-$90

1990's 4 Piece Decanter
Set
approx value $250-$500

1990's Collector Plate
approx value $25-$35

1980's Soup Bowl w/Lid
approx value $18-$30

1990's Coasters
approx value $25-$45

54

1990's Tea Pot Set
approx value $65-$100

1970's Coffee Pot
approx value $45-$65

1990's Ceramic Coffee Pot
approx value $85-$150

1990's Napkin Holder
approx value $65-$100

1990's Juice Carafe
approx value $45-$65

1990's Soup Cup
approx value $25-$45

DODGERS BLUE CREW

1990's Dodgers Sticker
approx value $15-$25

1990's Dodgers Blue Crew
Wallet
approx value $35-$45

1990's Dodgers Stickers
Holder with Coupons
approx value $15-$20

1990's Dodgers Blue Crew Hat
approx value $25-$45

1990's Dodgers Certificate
approx value $45-$65

1990's Dodgers Entry Form
Holder with Coupons
approx value $125-$225

1990's Dodgers Calender
approx value $25-$45

DOLLS

1970's Plush Nugget Doll
approx value $45-$85

1970's Plush Nugget Doll
approx value $85-$145

1970's Plush Dolly Doll
approx value $45-$85

1970's Plush Dolly Doll
approx value $85-$145

1970's Plush Bobs Doll
approx value $45-$85

1970's Plush Bobs Doll
approx value $85-$145

1970's Dakin Doll
approx value $50-$65

1970's Dakin Doll with
Black shoes
approx value $100-$225

1970's Dakin Doll with
Burger
approx value $100-$125

1990's Blow Up Doll
approx value $15-$25

1968-87 Plush Doll
approx value $25-$35

EMPLOYEE AND CORPORATE ITEMS

1994 Employees Guide
approx value $45-$65

1980's Food Safety Guild
approx value $35-$45

1950's Clipboard
approx value $100-$175

1970's Notebook Holder
approx value $45-$65

1990's Tip Guide Book -
yellow
approx value $50-$65

1990's Tip Guide Book-White
approx value $50-$65

1970's Waitress Book
approx value $25-$45

1960's Memo Pad
approx value $85-$100

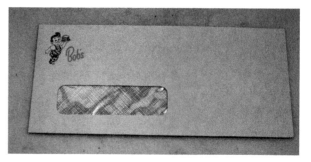

1970's Envelope
approx value $45-$65

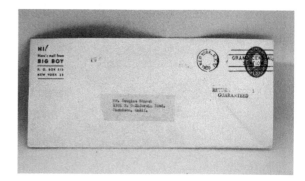

1959 Envelope
approx value $100-$150

1940's Laundry Card
approx value $300-$500

1980's Metal Plaque
approx value $200-$225

1969-87 Return Address
Label
approx value $65-$100

1969-87 Guest Receipt
Advertisement
approx value $65-$100

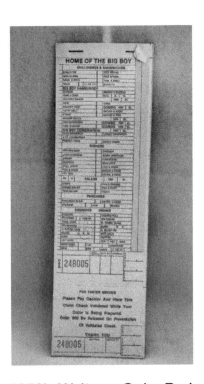

1950's Waitress Order Pad
approx value $100-$150

1980's Paper Hat
approx value $175-$250

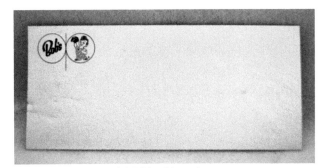

1950's Envelope
approx value $200-$225

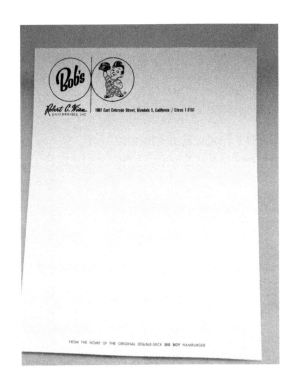

1950's Stationary
approx value $200-$250

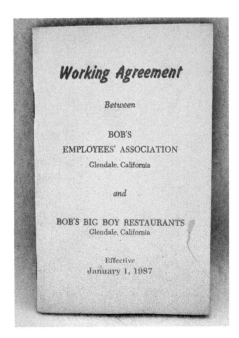

1987 Workers Agreement Book
approx value $150-$225

1969-87 Waitress Training
Book
approx value $225-$275

1966 Conference schedule
approx value $225-$275

1970's Maintenance Log
approx value $300-$375

1970's Food Bar Manual
approx value $300-$375

62   1970's Affirmative Action
approx value $300-$375

1970's Managers Manual
approx value $300-$375

1980's Training Letter
approx value $45-$65

1969-87 Car Hop
ID Badge
approx value $25-$35

1969-87 ID Badge
approx value $25-$35

1956-68 Letterhead
approx value $45-$65

1970's Business Card
approx value $45-$65

1980's ID Badge
approx value $15-$25

1973 Letter from corporation
approx value $45-$65

1970's Loss Prevention Book
approx value $65-$85

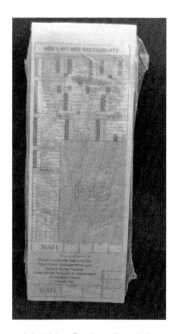

1970's Order Pad-full
approx value $85-$125

1990's Safe food certificate-approx value $45-$65
1969-87 Safety Book -approx value $145-$165
1969-87 Cashier Book-approx value $145-$165

1973 News Letter
approx value $125-$145

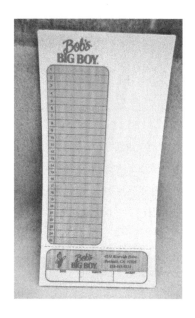

1969-87 Order Pad
approx value $145-$165

1970's Order Pad
approx value $50-$65

1990's Jobs Offers info
approx value $15-$25

1970's Representative Plaque
approx value $225-$300

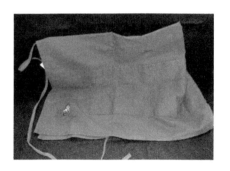

1970's Waitress Uniform
approx value $225-$300

1960's 48" round copper Wall Plaque
Commissioned by Ray Danner for corporate
office -Only 2 ever made
approx value $5000-$10000

1990's Waitress Apron
approx value $45-$55

1990's Menu Award
approx value $125-$185

1969-87 ID Badges
approx value $25-$35

1969-87 Employee of the
Month Wall Plaque
approx value $250-$350

1996 Uniform Bow Tie
approx value $25-$45

1969-87 Employee
Handbook
approx value $185-$225

1956-68 Employee
Handbook
approx value $285-$325

1956-68 Employee
Handbook
approx value $285-$325

FLOOR MATS

1956-68 Floor Mat
approx value $350-$450

1969-87 Welcome Mat
60" x 48"
approx value $185-$200

1956-68 Welcome Mat
48" x 36"
approx value $100-$185

1969-87 Welcome Mat
72" x 48'
approx value $200-$225

67

FOOD BAGS AND CONTAINERS

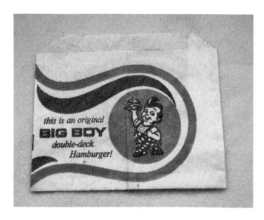

1956-68 Burger Bag
approx value $85-$145

1937-55 Burger Bag
approx value $200-$300

1937-55 Burger Bag
approx value $200-$300

1956-68 Burger Bag
approx value $85-$145

1956-68 Burger Bag
approx value $85-$145

1956-68 Burger Bag
approx value $50-$65

1969-87 Burger Bag
approx value $5-$8

1990's Fry Bag
approx value $5-$8

1937-55 Burger Bag
approx value $200-$300

1988-93 Bag
approx value $8-$15

approx value $8-$15
1988-93 French Fry Bag
approx value $5-$8

69

1956-68 Bag
approx value $65-$85

1990's Bag
approx value $8-$15

1990's Bag
approx value $8-$15

1990's Bag
approx value $8-$15

1968-87 Jelly Packets
approx value $8-$12

1988-93 Bag
approx value $8-$15

1969-87 Bag
approx value $25-$35

1969-87 Bag
approx value $25-$35

1956-68
approx value $50-$65

1969-87 Bag
approx value $25-$35

1969-87 Bag
approx value $25-$35

1990's Hamburger wrapper
approx value $8-$15

1969-87 Plastic To go Box
approx value $85-$125

1990's Coffee Cup Wrap
approx value $6-$12

1969-89 Mocha Boy
Coffee-Unopened
approx value $100-$200

1956-68 Mocha Boy
Coffee-Unopened
approx value $125-$225

1969-87 Instant Coffee
approx. value $15-$20

1969-87 Hot Chocolate
Fudge
approx value $100-$200

1969-87 To Go Cup
approx value $20-$35

1969-87 Pie Box
approx value $45-$65

1990's Kids Meal Box
approx value $18-$35

1990's Pie Box
approx value $15-$35

1969-87 Pie Box
approx value $45-$65

1956-68 Pie Pan
approx value $225-$400

73

 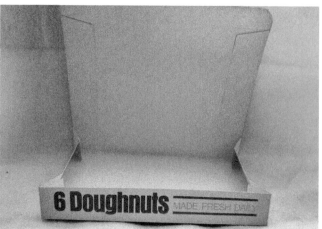

1969-87 Doughnuts Box
approx value $225-$325

1990's Kids Meal Box
approx value $18-$35

1956-68 Shrimp Box
approx value $285-$350

1956-68 Straw
approx value $25-$45

1980's Burger Wrap
approx value $8-$15

1990's To Go Bag
approx value $15-$25

1956-68 Dressing Box
approx value $65-$125

1969-87 Whipped Cream
Bottle
approx value $185-$225

1990's Kids Meal Bag
approx value $18-$35

GAMES AND TOYS

1970's Burbank Collector
Car
approx value $45-$65

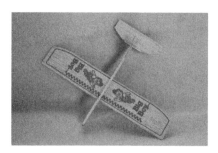

1969-88 Glider Plane
approx value $125-$165

1980's Antenna Ball
approx value $15-$25

1990's Burger Toss
Games Set
approx value $55-$85

1990's Sidewalk Chalk
approx value $8-$15

1990's Soft Frisbee
approx value $15-$25

1990's Checkers Game
approx value $8-$15

1969-87 Ruler
approx value $25-$35

76

1990's Folding Binoculars
approx value $8-$15

1990's Stencil Pencil set
approx value $15-$20

1990's Bendable Bob
approx value $8-$15

1960's Notebook
approx value $25-$35

1990's Punch-out Puppet
approx value $25-$35

1990's Pail and shovel
approx value $25-$35

1990's Inflatable Beach
Ball
approx value $10-$20

1980's Advertisement
approx value $50-$65

1990's Pail and shovel
78approx value $25-$35

1990's Pail and shovel
approx value $25-$35

1990's Big Boy & Pals
Puzzle
approx value $25-$35

1990's Big Boy & Pals
Puzzle
approx value $25-$35

1969-87 Puzzle
approx value $45-$65

1990's Big Boy & Pals
Puzzle
approx value $25-$35

1990's Big Boy & Pals
Puzzle
approx value $25-$35

1990's Black Coin Purse
approx value $25-$35

1990's Basketball Mini Game
approx value $8-$15

1969-87 Hand puppet
approx value $35-$45

1990's Pog Set #1
approx value $15-$25

1990's Pog Set #2
approx value $15-$25

1990's Rainbow Slinky
approx value $25-$35

1990's Sun Glasses
approx value $8-$15

1980's Note Pad
approx value $20-$30

1990's Pencil Box
approx value 215-$35

1990's Wallet
approx value $15-$35

1969-87 Photo Book
approx value $35-$45

1990's Color Dough
approx value $15-$25

1990's Plastic Yo-Yo approx value $8-$15
1960's Wooden Yo-Yo approx value $45-$55

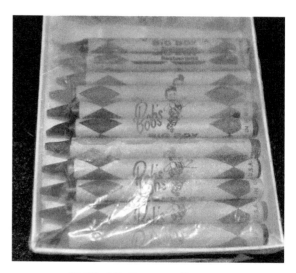

1969-87 Crayon Set
approx value $125-$200

1990's Frisbee
approx value $15-$25

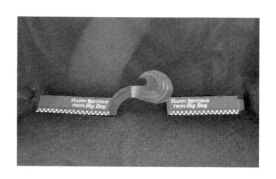

1990's Paper Headband
approx value $8-$15

1990's Crayon Set
approx value $50-$65

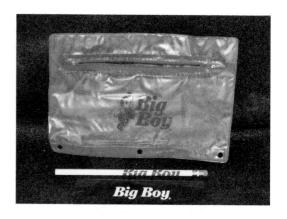

1990's Pencil Bag
approx value $15-$25

1990's Messenger Bag
approx value $35-$45

1990's Ruler
approx value $8-$15

1990's Coin Purse
approx value $8-$12

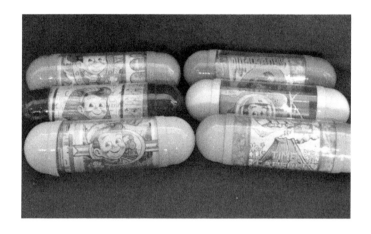

1990's Time Capsules
approx value $15-$25

1990's Checkered Coin
Purse
approx value $25-$35

1990's Round Coin Purse
approx value $25-$35

1990's Snow Globe
approx value $65-$85

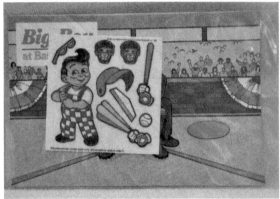

1990's Color Forms
approx value $35-$45

1990's Color Forms
approx value $35-$45

1956-68 Board Game
approx value $185-$225

1990's Color Forms
approx value $35-$45

1984 Plastic Action Figure
approx value $65-$85

2007 Coin Keeper
approx value $15-$25

1990's Action Figure Set
with Display
approx value $185-$225

2007 Coin Keeper
approx value $15-$25

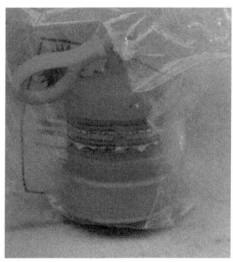

2007 Coin Keeper
approx value $15-$25

2007 Coin Keeper
approx value $15-$25

1990's Action Figure
approx value $5-$10

1990's Action Figure
approx value $5-$10

1990's Action Figure
approx value $5-$10

1990's Action Figure
approx value $5-$10

1990's Action Figure
approx value $5-$10

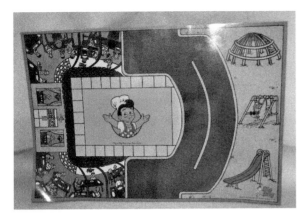

1990's Car Track Place
mat
approx value $15-$25

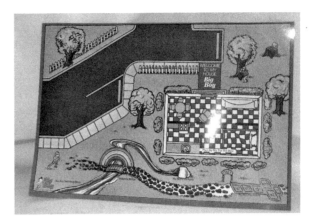

1990's Car Track Place
mat
approx value $15-$25

1990's Car Track Place
mat
approx value $15-$25

1990's Car Track Place
mat
approx value $15-$25

1990's Car Track Place
mat
approx value $15-$25

GOLF

1969-88 Golf Tags
approx value $85-$125

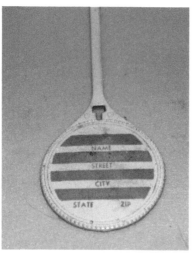

1969-88 Golf Tags
approx value $85-$125

1969-88 Golf Tags
approx value $85-$125

1969-87 Golf Ball Place
marker
approx value $85-$125

1990's Golf ball-Tee Set
approx value $85-$125

1980's Golf Tee Set
approx value $45-$65

1969-87 Orange Gold Ball
approx value $25-$35

88

HALLOWEEN

1969-87 Trick or Treat
Coupon Book
approx value $65-$85

1969-87 Tick or Treat Bag
approx value $35-$45

1990's Trick or Treat
Bucket
approx value $18-$35

1980's Advertisement
approx value $50-$65

1969-87 Treat Coupons
approx value $25-$35

1969-87 Mask coupon set
approx value $45-$65

JEWELRY

1956-67 Tie Tack
approx value $65-$85

1956-67 Key Chain
approx value $65-$85

1988-93 Plastic Ring
approx value $6-$10

1956-68 Neckerchief Tie
approx value $285-$325

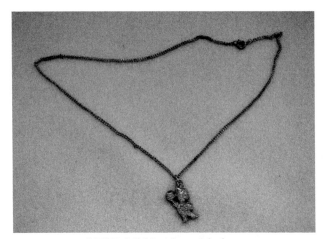

1956-68 Neckerchief
approx value $65-$85

1956-68 Pin
approx value $45-$65

1969-87 Metal Key Chain
approx value $25-$35

1990's Plastic Key Chain
approx value $6-$8

1969-87 Metal Key Chain
approx value $45-$65

1969-87 Plastic Key Chain
approx value $6-$8

1956-68 Cuff Links
approx value $125-$185

1969-87 Zippo Key Chain
approx value $185-$225

1969-87 Neckerchief Tie
approx value $285-$325

1990's Plastic Key chain
approx value $8-$15

1956-68 Pin
approx value $45-$65

1956-68 Tie Tack
approx value $125-$185

1988-93 Key chain Knife
approx value $85-$125

1956-68 Clip On Ear rings
approx value $125-$165

1969-87 Outstanding
Service Pin
approx value $65-$85

1990's Key Chain
approx value $25-$35

1969-87 3 year
Anniversary Pin
approx value $65-$125

1969-87 Money Clip
approx value $45-$65

1988-96 Leather Key Ring
approx value $45-$85

1990's Earring Studs
approx value $25-$35

1990's Hanging Earrings
approx value $25-$35

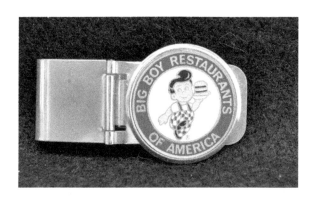

1969-87 Money Clip
approx value $125-$165

1956-68 Money Clip
approx value $145-$185

KIDS CLUB

1960 Membership Card
approx value $35-$45

1990's Membership Card
approx value $15-$25

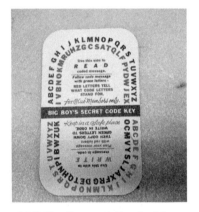

1950's Secret Code Key
approx value $30-$45

1966 Membership Card
approx value $35-$45

1950's Club Membership
approx value $45-$65

1950's Secret Code Letter
approx value $85-$125

1956-68 Post Card
approx value $35-$45

1959 Membership Sticker
approx value $65-$85

1969-87 Postcard
approx value $20-$30

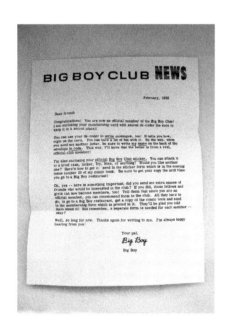

1959 Club Letter
approx value $85-$125

1950's Pennants Flag -approx value $125-$165
1990's Pennants Flag-approx value $25-$45

LIGHTERS

1996 Limited Edition of
1000 Zippo Lighter
approx value $185-$225

1990's Brass limited Edition of
500 Zippo Lighter
approx value $225-$300

1990's Lighter
approx value $85-$145

1990's Lighter
approx value $85-$145

1990's Lighter
approx value $85-$145

1950's Lighter-White
approx value $225-$300

1950's Lighter-White
approx value $225-$300

1969-87 Plastic Lighter
approx value $85-$125

1990's Set of Lighter
approx value $125-$185

LIGHTS AND LAMPS

1969-87 Night Light
approx value $125-$165

1990's Pen Light
approx value $5-$15

1956-68 Lamp
approx value $3000-$6000

1990's Lamp
approx value $625-$1000

1990's Night Light
approx value $15-$25

1990 Large Night Light
approx value $65-$85

1956-68 Night Light in Box
98
approx value $325-$400

MAGNETS

1969-87 Magnet
approx value $8-$15

1969-87 Magnet
approx value $8-$15

1969-87 Magnet
approx value $8-$15

1988-93 Magnet
approx value $8-$15

1988-93 Magnet
approx value $8-$15

1990's Magnet
approx value $8-$15

MATCHBOOKS

1930's Match Book
approx value $85-$125

1930's Match Book
approx value $225-$265

1937-55 Match Book
approx value $85-$125

1937-55 Match Book
Back and Front views
approx value $85-$125

1937-55 Match Book
approx value $85-$125

1937-55 Match Book
approx value $125-$145

1956-68 Wood Match Box
approx value $85-$125

1956-68 Match Book
approx value $25-$45

1937-55 Match Book
approx value $85-$125

1937-56 Match Book
approx value $85-$125

1969-87 Match Book
approx value $5-$15

1969-87 Match Book
approx value $5-$15

1969-87 Match Book
approx value $5-$15

1956-68 Match Book
approx value $85-$125

1956-68 Match Book
approx value $85-$125

1956-68 Match Book
approx value $85-$125

1956-68 Match Book
approx value $85-$125

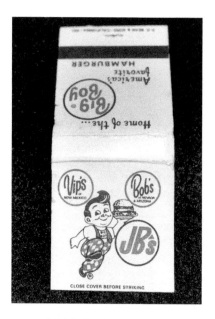

1969-87 Match Book
approx value $5-$15

1956-68 Match Book
approx value $45-$65

1956-68 Match Book
approx value $45-$65

1969-87 Match Book
approx value $5-$15

1956-67 Match Book
approx value $85-$125

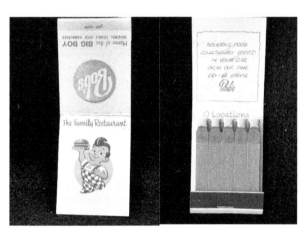

1956-68 Match Book
approx value $125-$145

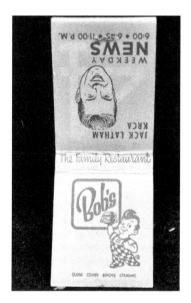

1956-68 Match Book
approx value $45-$65

1956-68 Match Book
approx value $45-$65

1956-68 Match Book
approx value $125-$145

MENUS

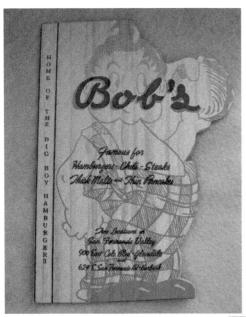

1930's First Menu Made
approx value $225-$400

1990's Breakfast Menu
approx value $25-$45

1990's Menu
approx value $25-$45

1990's Menu
104approx value $25-$45

1990's Desert Menu
approx value $25-$45

1990's Desert Menu
approx value $25-$45

1990's Breakfast Menu
approx value $25-$45

1988-96 Menu
approx value $25-$45

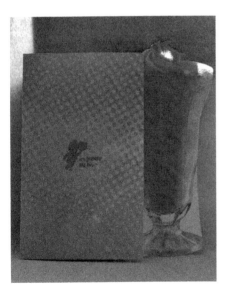

1990's Menu
approx value $25-$45

1990's Menu
approx value $25-$45

1990's Menu
approx value $25-$45

1956-68 To Go Menu
approx value $65-$85

1949 Menu
approx value $85-$125

1956-86 Menu
approx value $85-$125

1969-87 Menu
approx value $45-$65

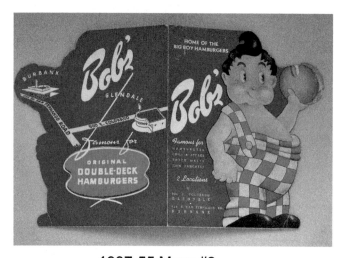

1937-55 Menu #2
approx value $225-$300

1969-87 Menu
approx value $125-$145

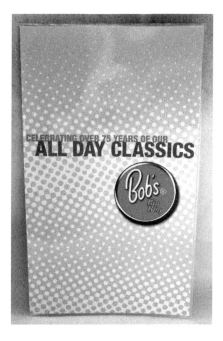

1969-87 Menu
approx value $45-$87

1937-55 Breakfast Menu
approx value $185-$225

1990's Menu
approx value $45-$65

1990's Menu
approx value $85-$125

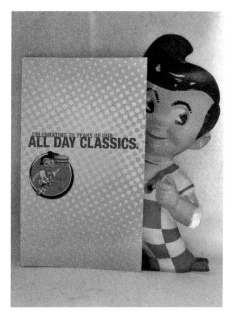

1969-87 Menu
approx value $85-$125

1990's Take Out Menu
approx value $5-$15

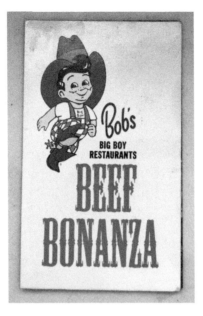

1980's Menu
approx value $185-$225

2006 Menu
approx value $65-$85

1969-87 Breakfast Menu
approx value $125-$165

1990's Menu
approx value $25-$35

1988-96 Burbank To Go
Menu
approx value $25-$45

1990's Breakfast Menu
approx value $65-$85

1970's Breakfast Menu
approx value $65-$85

1990's Menu
approx value $25-$35

1969-87 Menu
approx value $45-$65

1969-87 Menu
approx value $85-$125

1970's Menu
approx value $65-$85

1990's Kids Menu
approx value $25-$45

1990's Menu
approx value $25-$45

1990's Desert Menu
approx value $45-$65

1990's Menu
approx value $25-$45

1990's Take Out Menu
approx value $5-$8

1990's Desert Menu
approx value $15-$25

1990's Menu
approx value $15-$25

1990's Menu
approx value $65-$85

1990's Desert Menu
approx value $15-$25

1969-87 Take Out Menu
approx value $65-$85

1990's Menu
approx value $185-$225

1990's Menu
approx value $185-$225

1990's Menu
approx value $185-$225

1990's Menu
approx value $185-$225

1950's Take Out Menu
approx value $125-$165

1990's Menu
approx value $65-$85

1990's Advertisement
approx value $65-$85

1956-68 Menu
approx value $225-$265

1956-68 Menu
approx value $225-$265

1956-68 Menu
approx value $225-$265

1940's Menu
approx value $125-$165

1939 Menu
approx value $245-$285

1940's Menu
approx value $165-$225

1939 Menu
approx value $265-$285

1969-87 Menu
approx value $125-$145

1970's Menu
approx value $65-$85

1990's Menu
approx value $65-$85

1969-87 Menu
approx value $225-$300

1969-87 Menu
approx value $125-$165

1960's Prototype Menu
approx value $285-$325

1990's Menu
approx value $65-$85

1988-96 Menu
approx value $65-$85

1956-68 Take Out Menu
approx value $125-$165

1993 Menu
approx value $65-$85

1990's Burbank Menu
approx value $25-$45

1956-68 Breakfast Menu
approx value $165-$225

1990's Pie Menu
approx value $25-$65

1950's Menu
approx value $225-$265

1970's Menu
approx value $125-$145

1980's Children's Menu
approx value $25-$45

1988-96 Kids Menu
approx value $15-$25

2000's Menu
approx value $15-$65

1970's Menu
approx value $45-$65

1970's Canadian Menu
Written in French
approx value $285-$300

1993 Menu
approx value $45-$65

1969-87 Breakfast Menu
Written In Japanese
approx value $285-$300

1960's Braille Menu
approx value $300-$500

1950's Take Out Menu
Board
approx value $255-$300

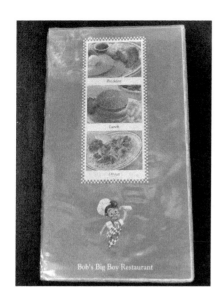

1969-87 Menu
approx value $85-$65

1990's Menu Board
approx value $45-$65

1988-96 Menu Board
approx value $45-$65

1990's Burbank Menu
approx value $65-$85

1990's Desert Menu
approx value $45-$65

1990's Desert Menu
approx value $45-$65

1969-87 Menu
approx value $45-$65

MISCELLANEOUS

1969-87 Produce Box
approx value $300-$500

1969-87 Big Boy Knife
approx value $300-$500

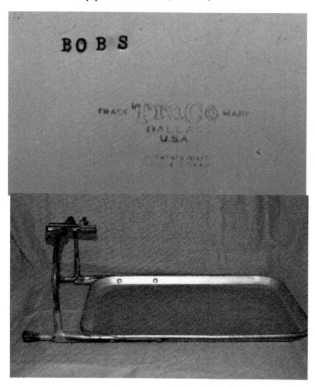

1969-87 Plaque
Hung in Corporate Office
approx value $550-$650

1950's Car Hop Tray
Stamped with Bobs onto it
approx value $185-$250

1956-68 Toothpicks
approx value $5-$10 each

1969-87 Shoe Horn
approx value $85-$125

1969-87 Can Radio
approx value $2000-$3000

1970's Oops Card
approx value $25-$35

1990's Tooth Pick Holder
approx value $65-$85

1969-87 Metal Corporate
Plaque
approx value $165-$185

2000's Lanyard
approx value $5-$12

1969-87 Road Map Holder
approx value $65-$85

1970's Pewter Card Holder
approx value $185-$225

1990's Greeting Card
approx value $15-$25

1930's Burger Press
approx value $285-$325

1969-87 Cardboard Card
approx value $25-$35

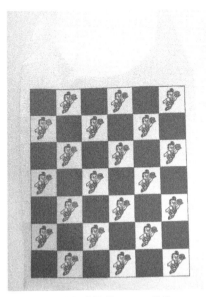

1969-87 Paper Bib
approx value $65-$85

1969-87 Ribbon
approx value $15-$25

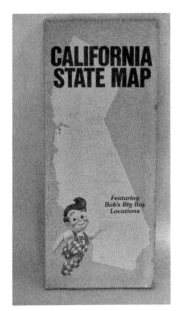

1969-87 Map
approx value $65-$85

1960's Paper Bib
approx value $65-$85

1956-68 Prototype Bib
approx value $185-$225

1956-68 Perfumes
approx value $125-$165

1968-87 Bobs Big Boy Blue Prints
Calabasas Restaurant
approx value $600-$1000

1990's Newspaper Stand
Front Panel
approx value $285-$350

1990's Lunch Box
approx value $65-$85

1999 Limited Edition Rocket Boy Cell
with Certificate
approx value $185-$225

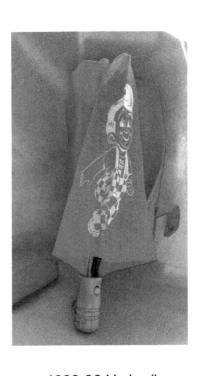

1988-96 Umbrella
approx value $125-$145

1990's Plastic Crate
approx value $45-$65

1956-68 Stencil negative
for Ashtrays
approx value $350-$425

1956-68 Printers Block
approx value $185-$225

1956-68 Printers Block
approx value $185-$225

1956-68 Printers Block
approx value $185-$225

1990's Hand Sanitizer
approx value $25-$45

1990's Decorative Skillet
with Holder
approx value $85-$125

1990's Envelopes
approx value $8-$15

2000 Burger Boy New Letter
approx value $8-$15

1970's Ballot to Retire
Big Boy
approx value $25-$45

2000 Burger Boy News
Subscription Form
approx value $8-$15

1990's Scale HO Model
approx value $225-$350

1990's Scale HO Model
approx value $225-$350

1990's Tool Kit
approx value $85-$125

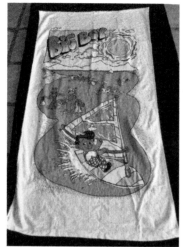

1990's Beach Towel
approx value $25-$35

1969-87 Big Boy Fabric
approx value $25-$35

1960's Radio Commercials
approx value $265-$325

1960's Employees Training
Record and Film Slides
approx value $285-$325

1950's Radio Spots with
Bob Hope
approx value $850-$1000

1998 Car Show Plaque
approx value $8-$15

1990's Packaging Guide
approx value $45-$65

1990's Sugar Cookie
approx value $25-$35

1990's Accident Score Board
approx value $25-$35

1969-87 Plastic Crate
approx value $185-$225

1956-68 Wet Paint Sign
approx value $125-$185

1969-87 Costume
approx value $1000-$1500

1990's Cells from Last Commercial made
approx value $225-$265 each

1990's Book Cover
approx value $15-$25

1990's Tooth Pick Holder
approx value $25-$45

PAPPY PARKER

1970's Pappy Parker Figurines
approx value $65-$85 each

1970's Pappy Parker Menu
approx value $45-$65

PATCHES

1969-87 BBRA Patch
approx value $18-$25

1990's Patch
approx value $18-$25

1990's Patch
approx value $18-$25

1990's Patch
approx value $18-$25

PENS, PENCILS AND RULERS

1988-96 Evolution Pens
approx value $45-$65

1990's Pen
approx value $8-$15

1969-87 Pen
approx value $15-$25

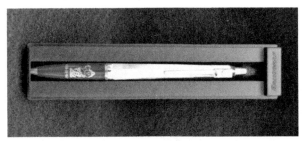

1970's Ball Point Pen
approx value $25-$35

1990's Figurine Pen
approx value $15-$25

1969-87 Pen Set
approx value $125-$145

1990's Bic Pen
approx value $4-$8

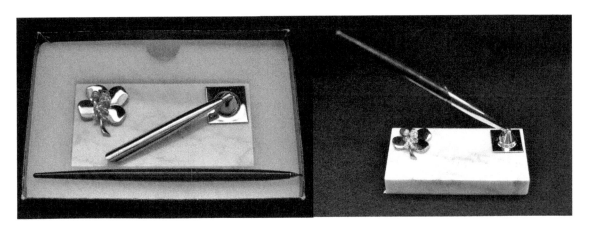

1970's Corporate Pen Set
approx value $285-$325

1990's Pen & Paper Set
approx value $25-$35

1990's Ceramic Bob Pen Set
approx value $385-$425

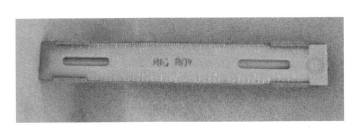

1990's Ruler Pencil Box
approx value $25-$35

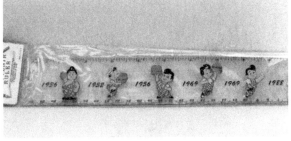

1990's Evolution Ruler
approx value $10-$15

PINS AND BUTTONS

1969-88 Birthday Club
approx value $20-$30

1990's Pin
approx value $8-$15

1969-87 Big Boy Buddy
Button
approx value $25-$35

1950's Waitress Pin
approx value $35-$45

1969-87 Members Pin
approx value $20-$25

134

1960's Big Boy Club Pin
approx value $20-$30

1970's Corporate name
Badge Pin
approx value $800-$1000

1970's Employee Pin
approx value $25-$35

1990's Desert Pin
approx value $8-$15

1988-96 Star Pin
approx value $25-$35

1956-68 Ribbon Pin
approx value $45-$65

1970's #1 Pin
approx value $25-$35

1987 Collector Pin
approx value $25-$35

1969-87 Service Pin
approx value $45-$65

1970's Brass Bobs Pin
approx value $25-$35

1969-87 Service Pin
approx value $45-$65

1970's Pin
approx value $18-$20

1969-87 Seafood Pin
approx value $40-$65

1988-96 Pin
approx value $25-$35

1990's Pin
approx value $15-$25

1990's Pin
approx value $8-$15

1950's Pin
approx value $15-$20

1960's Pin Set
approx value $225-$285

1956-68 Pin
approx value $25-$45

1969-87 Pin
approx value $25-$45

1980's Advertisement
approx value $50-$65

2002 Rose Parade Pin
approx value $8-$15

1990's Safety Program Pin
approx value $15-$25

1956-68 Pin
approx value $65-$85

1990's Flying Ace Pin
approx value $25-$45

1980's Strawberry Pin
approx value $15-$25

1969-87 Pin
approx value $15-$25

1970's Pin
approx value $20-$30

1990's Bake Shop Pin
approx value $15-$20

1990's Collector Pin
approx value $15-$20

1990's Collector Pin
approx value $15-$20

1990's Collector Pin
approx value $15-$20

1969-87 Collector Pin
approx value $15-$20

1990's Collector Pin
approx value $15-$20

1990's Hot Rod Pin
approx value $15-$20

1970 Pin
approx value $25-$35

1990 Pin
approx value $20-$30

1969-87 Pin
approx value $25-$25

1988-96 Pin
approx value $15-$20

1988-96 Pin
approx value $20-$25

1988-96 Pin
approx value $20-$25

1969-87 Pin
approx value $25-$45

Bob Wian To City
Council Pin
approx value $5000-$8000

1990's Pin
approx value $15-$25

1988-96 President Pin
approx value $15-$45

1970 Veg Pin
approx value $25-$35

1970 Desert Pin
approx value $25-$35

SALT AND PEPPER SHAKERS

1990's Salt & Pepper Shaker
approx value $65-$125

1990's Salt & Pepper Shaker
approx value $65-$125

1990's Salt & Pepper Shaker
approx value $65-$125

1990's Salt & Pepper Shaker
approx value $65-$125

1990's Salt & Pepper Shaker
approx value $65-$125

1990's Salt & Pepper Shaker
approx value $65-$125

1990's Salt & Pepper Shaker
approx value $65-$125

1990's Salt & Pepper Shaker
approx value $65-$125

1990's Salt & Pepper Shaker
approx value $65-$125

1990's Salt & Pepper Shaker
approx value $65-$125

1990's Salt & Pepper Shaker
approx value $65-$125

1990's Salt & Pepper Shaker
approx value $65-$125

1990's Salt & Pepper Shaker
approx value $125-$145

1956-68 Salt & Pepper
Shaker
approx value $45-$65

1956-68 Salt & Pepper Shaker
approx value $45-$65

1956-68 Salt & Pepper Shaker
approx value $45-$65

SEASONING

1950's Seasoning Salt
approx. value $65-$85

1950's Seasoning Salt
approx. value $65-$85

1956-68 Roquefort Dressing
approx. value $65-$85

1956-68 Seasoning Salt
approx. value $65-$85

1956-68 Blue Cheese
approx. value $65-$85

1956-68 1000 Island
approx. value $00-$00

1969-87 Seasoning Salt
approx. value $25-$35

1956-68 Strawberry Glaze
approx. value $65-$85

1956-68 Roquefort Dressing
approx. value $650-$85

1956-68 French Dressing
approx. value $65-$85

1600's Tartar Sauce Jar
approx. value $45-$65

1956-68 Roquefort Dressing
approx. value $65-$85

1950's Relish Jar
approx. value $65-$85

1990's Sugar Packs
approx. value $2-$5

1956-68 Sugar Pack
approx. value $25-$45

1937-55 Sugar Cube
approx. value $125-$185

1969-87 Salt & Pepper
approx. value $65-$85

1969-88 Sugar Packs
approx. value $25-$35

1990's Artificial Sugar Packs
approx. value $2-$5

1956-68 Salt Packs
approx. value $45-$65

SENIORS

2000's Senior Card
approx. value $3-$5

1990's Senior Card
approx. value $10-$15

1969-87 Senior Card
approx. value $45-$65

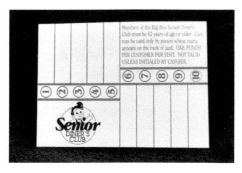

1969-87 Senior Card
approx. value $15-$20

1969-87 Senior Card
approx. value $25-$35

SIGNS AND BANNERS

1950's Closed Section Sign
approx. value $45-$65

1988-96 Combo Banner
approx. value $85-$125
1969-87 Breakfast Banner
approx. value $125-$200
1969-87 Breakfast Banner
approx. value $125-$200

1988-96 Combo Banner
approx. value $85-$125
1988-96 President Banner
approx. value $225-$325
1969-87 Patriotism Banner
approx. value $225-$325

1969-87 Combo Banner -approx. value $225-$325
1969-87 Twilight Banner -approx. value $225-$325
1969-87 Breakfast Banner -approx. value $225-$325

1988-96 Menu Board
approx. value $185-$225

1988-96 Wood Hat Sign
approx. value $285-$325

1950's Tops Sign- We have not yet located the
Bobs Sign
approx. value $5000-$8000

1988-96 Menu Board
approx. value $185-$225

1990's 8' Neon Store front Sign from Victorville
Bobs Big Boy
approx. value $800-$1500

1970's Neon sign from the
inside lobby of Bobs Big Boy 151
approx. value $2500-$3000

1988-96 Refreshment Banner -approx. value $85-$125
1969-87 Chicken Banner -approx. value $125-$185
1969-87 Combo Banner -approx. value $125-$185

1956-68 Direction Banner
approx. value $325-$425

1990's Bill Board Sign
approx. value $800-$1000

1968-87 Neon Sign from The
Burbank Bobs Bog Boy
approx. value $8000-$10000

1990's Neon Sign
approx. value $400-$600

1990's Bill Board Sign
approx. value $600-$800

1969-87 Wooden Sign-Only 2
ever made-Came off the Bobs
Fair Trailer
approx. value $4000-$6000

1990's Menu Chalk Board
approx. value $25-$45

1956-68 Plastic Sign
approx. value $1500-$2500

1990's Neon Sign
approx. value $2500-$4000

1970's Enter Sign
approx. value $800-$1200

1990's Restroom Signs
approx. value $225-$325

STATUES

1956-68 Corporate Statue with Original crown- given out at the Big Boy Restaurants of America Conference
approx. value $8000-$15000

1950's Plastic Big Boy Statue
approx. value $15-$25

1960 Teeny Tiny Big Boy Statue
approx. value $45-$65

1990's Big Boy Statue
approx. value $85-$125

1956-68 Employee Award Statue
approx. value $185-$250

1969-87 4' Statue
approx. value $600-$800

1969-87 4' Statue
approx. value $600-$800

1950's Paper mache Counter
top Statue
approx. value $2500-$5000

Big Boy Collection
Limited copper Edition series #1
1 of 500
"1936"
Fine Pewter Made in USA
approx value $15-$35

Big Boy Collection
Limited Edition series #1
1 of 500
"1936"
Fine Pewter Made in USA
approx value $15-$35

Big Boy Collection
Limited Edition series #2
1 of 500
"1956"
Fine Pewter Made in
USA
approx value $15-$35

Big Boy Collection
Limited Edition series #3
1 of 500
"1969"
Fine Pewter Made in USA
approx value $15-$35

Big Boy Collection
Limited Edition series #4
1 of 500
"1969"
Fine Pewter Made in USA
approx value $15-$35

1956-68 Plaster Statue
w/blue eyes
approx. value $285-$325

1956-68 Corporate Bookend
Statue
approx. value $525-$650

1956-68 Plaster Statue
approx. value $285-$325

1956-68 Brass Bank Mold
Statue
approx. value $385-$425

STICKERS AND TATTOOS

1956-68 Sticker
approx. value $45-$65

1988-96 Sticker
approx. value $25-$35

1969-88 Direction Banner
approx. value $25-$35

1988-96 Decal
approx. value $25-$35

1956-68 Sticker
approx. value $45-$65

1936-55 Decal
approx. value $85-$125

1988-96 Sticker
approx. value $15-$20

1990's Decal
approx. value $15-$20

1969-87 Assorted Bumper
Stickers
approx. value $15-$25

1990's Bake Shop Sticker
approx. value $10-$15

1969-87 Sticker Sheet
approx. value $15-$25

1990's Sticker Album
approx. value $25-$35

1990's Sticker Sheet
approx. value $5-$15

1969-87 Rubber Sticker
Mold
approx. value $25-$35

TABLE TENTS

1956-68 Table Tent
approx. value $185-$225

1956-68 Table Tent
approx. value $185-$225

1969-87 Table Tent
approx. value $35-$45

1969-87 Table Tent
approx. value $185-$225

1990's Table Tent
approx. value $15-$25

1950's Table Tent
approx. value $250-$285

1950's Table Tent
approx. value $250-$285

1969-87 Table Tent
approx. value $45-$65

1950's Table Tent
approx. value $250-$285

1950's Table Tent
approx. value $250-$285

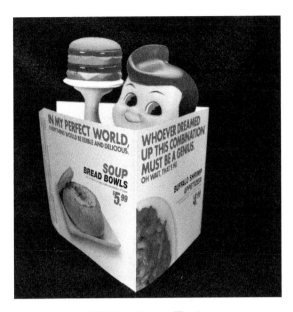

1990's Table Tent
approx. value $15-$25

1969-87 Table Tent
approx. value $20-$35

1990's Table Tent
approx. value $15-$20

1990's Table Tent
approx. value $15-$25

1988-96 Table Tent
approx. value $10-$15

1990's Table Tent
approx. value $5-$15

1950's Table Tent
approx. value $165-$225

1990's Table Tent
approx. value $5-$15

1969-87 Table Tent
approx. value $25-$35

1990's Table Tent
approx. value $5-$15

1990's Table Tent
approx. value $15-$20

1990's Table Tent
approx. value $5-$15

1990's Table Tent
approx. value $15-$25

1969-87 Table Tent
approx. value $25-$45

1956-68 Table Tent
approx. value $85-$125

1990's Table Tent
approx. value $65-$85

1950's Table Tent
approx. value $85-$125

1969-87 Table Tent
approx. value $45-$65

1990's Table Tent
approx. value $25-$45

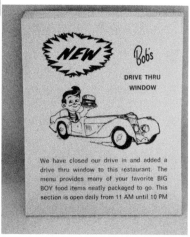

1956-68 Table Tent
approx. value $125-$185

1969-87 Table Tent
approx. value $15-$25

1990's Table Tent
approx. value $5-$15

1969-87 Table Tent
approx. value $15-$25

1990's Table Tent
approx. value $5-$15

1950's Table Tent
approx. value $85-$125

1990's Table Tent
approx. value $25-$45

TRADING CARDS

1976 Advertisement
approx. value $25-$45

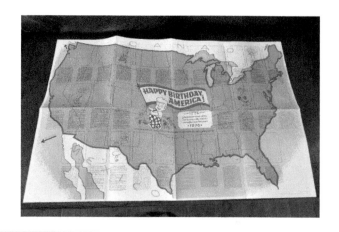

1976 Map
approx. value $185-$250

1976 Advertisement
approx. value $25-$45

1976 Advertisement
approx. value $25-$45

1976 Trading Cards Set
approx. value $225-$285

WAITRESS CARD

1930's Waitress Card
approx. value $285-$325

1950's Waitress Card
approx. value $185-$225

WATCHES

1990's Plastic Watch
approx. value $85-$125

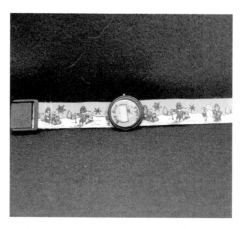

1990's Plastic Winter Watch
approx. value $85-$125

1990's Plastic Watch
approx. value $85-$125

1969-87 Leather Watch
approx. value $185-$225

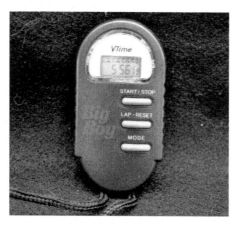

1990's Stop Watch
approx. value $125-$165

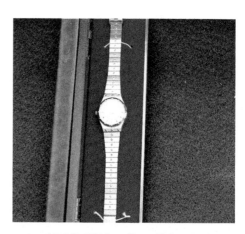

1969-87 Ladies Watch
approx. value $220-$265

1969-88 Watch
approx. value $285-$325

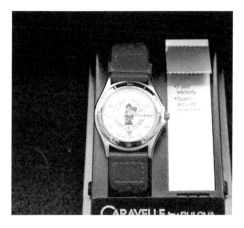

1988-96 Watch
approx. value $285-325

1969-87 Metal Watch
approx. value $125-$185

1988-96 Swatch Watch
approx. value $85-$125

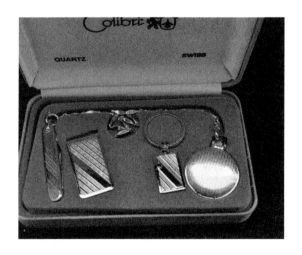

1969-87 Pocket Watch Set
approx. value $385-$425

1969-87 Bulova Watch
approx. value $185-$225

CPSIA information can be obtained at www.ICGtesting.com
Printed in the USA
BVOW11*1536180615

405023BV00010B/41/P